Old Iona and Staffa

by Bernard Byrom

Being a small island, Iona has always been totally dependent on receiving vital supplies by sea from Mull or the mainland. It used to be the practice for small coasters known as 'puffers' to sail into Port nam Mairtear (Martyrs' Bay), a little way south of the landing place, and beach at high tide. At low tide the villagers would go to the bay and unload their supplies from the ship, which would then refloat at the next high tide. This practice persisted until around the 1970s. The picture shows supplies being unloaded in Martyrs' Bay from the coaster *Spartan* and by now the villagers have the luxury of tractor-drawn trailers; in earlier days off-loading would have been by horse and cart. The bay's name refers to the slaughter here of 68 monks by the Vikings in AD 806.

First published in the United Kingdom, 2007,
reprinted 2012
by Stenlake Publishing Ltd.
www.stenlake.co.uk
ISBN 9781840334067

In this late-Victorian view of the beginning of the main street of Iona looking towards the abbey, the village shows a very neat and tidy appearance; today it would be a contender for the 'Best Kept Village' award. Although the island was dependent on tourism and pilgrims for its prosperity, the two-storey houses have a fine and solid appearance, and the people in the picture appear to be residents and look comfortably well-dressed. Notice that the roadway separates the houses from their gardens, which are on the seaward side of the road, just as it does today. The nearest semi-detached houses on the left are Block House and Roseneath.

INTRODUCTION

The island of Staffa was formed about 60 million years ago at a time of great volcanic activity in the west of Scotland. A huge swathe of lava poured westwards into the sea and solidified; at that time it stretched from Mull to Antrim in Northern Ireland. Over the next few million years most of this solidified lava eroded away and was covered by the sea, but a few outcrops remained as islands. Off the west coast of Scotland these were represented by Staffa, the Treshnish Islands and a few others. The other end of the lava field can be found in the Giant's Causeway in County Antrim, Northern Ireland.

Staffa is the most notable and unique of these Scottish islands. Geologically it is made up of three different types of rock. The lowest layer is called tuff and is composed of compressed volcanic ash and dust which would have been thrown from the volcanoes when they began to erupt. The middle layer is the lava which, as it cooled, formed itself into hexagonal basalt columns. Some of these are vertical but others have been compressed and twisted into fantastic shapes by the earth's movements over millions of years. Yet more columns have been broken off at different heights and, when seen from above, appear like a giant patchwork quilt. The tall basalt columns on the island are covered by a thick layer of volcanic debris mixed with pieces of broken columns which, in turn, is covered with rich soil and grass.

Since the island was formed, it has developed a west-to-east slope of around 4 degrees, which has lifted the tuff on its western side above sea level. As the tuff is geologically the weakest of the three rock layers, this is where the sea has broken in and over centuries has broken many of the basalt columns which once rested on the tuff. This has created the three great caves on the south-west corner of the island: Clamshell Cave, Fingal's Cave and Cormorant Cave.

The island is only three-quarters of a mile long and a quarter of a mile wide. Its circumference is $1\frac{1}{2}$ miles, its area is 71 acres and its highest point, Meall nam Gamhna, is 135 feet above sea level. The name Staffa is Norse, meaning Pillar Island, which obviously refers to its great pillars of basalt. Although the island had existed for millions of years and was well known to the local people, their very familiarity with it, coupled with its remoteness, ensured that its unique features were unknown to the outside world until 1772.

The three geological layers of Staffa. The tall basalt columns are known as the Colonnade and rise up to 56 feet in height.

Joseph Banks, a 25-year-old scientist, had headed a team of fellow scientists on Captain Cook's first voyage of exploration in 1768–71 to study the plants and rock structures in the southern hemisphere. When the explorers discovered Australia, Cook was so impressed by Banks's work there that he named Botany Bay in recognition of it. In August 1772 Banks set off to carry out scientific studies in Iceland, but on the way his ship was forced by bad weather to shelter in the Sound of Mull and he was entertained ashore. Here he was told of an island off the west coast of Mull with great pillars of rock, greater even than the Giant's Causeway. Next morning he sailed out to visit the island and was almost overwhelmed by its magnificence. When he returned home after his expedition to Iceland he wrote the following description of it in the *Scots Magazine*: 'Staffa, which is reckoned one of the greatest natural curiosities in the world, is surrounded by many pillars of different shapes such as pentagons, octagons, etc. There is a cave in this island which the natives call the Cave of Fingal: the whole sides are solid rock, and the bottom is covered with water 12 feet deep. The Giant's Causeway in Ireland, or Stonehenge in England, are but trifles when compared to this island.'

Banks's description of Staffa aroused a great deal of interest, not only in

Britain but also on the continent. Other travellers visited the island and wrote eloquent descriptions of its grandeur which, in turn, brought more and more tourists to the area. The neighbouring island of Iona had long been a place of pilgrimage and now both islands became the subject of an infant tourist industry.

Among Staffa's early would-be visitors were Dr Johnson and James Boswell, who planned to visit the island during their tour of Scotland in 1773 but were thwarted by the weather. Even today, visitors can only land when the sea is very calm with practically no swell.

The early years of the nineteenth century saw the beginning of the Romantic movement which swept across Europe. Great literary figures came to visit Scotland. Sir Walter Scott visited Staffa twice, in 1810 and 1814, and other famous visitors were the poets John Keats, William Wordsworth and Alfred, Lord Tennyson. On Wordsworth's visit in 1833 he grumbled about the number of tourists, a complaint that was echoed by Tennyson, who visited twenty years later. In 1830 a visit by the great English impressionist painter J. M. W. Turner resulted in two famous paintings, and in 1859 Jules Verne called at Staffa and later set the climax of his romantic novel *Le Rayon vert* (*The Green Ray*) on the island.

In 1847 the young Queen Victoria with Prince Albert, the Prince of Wales and the Princess Royal sailed in the royal yacht to Staffa, where they anchored and were rowed into Fingal's Cave. The Queen was very impressed, writing in her *Journal*: 'The appearance it presents is most extraordinary; and when we turned the corner to go into the renowned Fingal's Cave the effect was splendid, like a great entrance into a vaulted hall: it looked almost awful as we entered and the barge heaved up and down on the swell of the sea.'

The entrance to Fingal's Cave with the islet called the Herdsman in the distance, 1884.

But the person who has probably left us with the deepest impression of Fingal's Cave is the twenty-year-old Felix Mendelssohn, who visited Staffa on 8 August 1829 with his friend Karl Klingemann. It was not a pleasant journey: the sea was rough and Mendelssohn was horribly seasick, but he was so moved by the grandeur of the cave and the sounds made by the waves surging into it that fragments of music came into his mind, from which he composed his overture *Die Hebriden* (*The Hebrides*), which was subtitled *Fingal's Cave*. This powerfully evocative music has been popular ever since, but it's lucky that Mendelssohn was able to keep the main theme in his head for a few days; it is said that when he returned to the mainland he sat down at a piano to try out the theme but was firmly reminded that it was the Sabbath Day, so playing the piano was out of the question!

Staffa was continuously inhabited until 1798. When the French geologist Faujas visited in 1784 he found sixteen people living on the island in two huts built out of unhewn blocks of basalt roofed over with sods. Their livestock consisted of eight cows, one bull, twelve sheep, two horses, one pig, two dogs, one cock and eight hens. For about ten years after 1798, herdsmen and their families only lived on the island from spring to autumn; after around 1810 they departed for good, leaving their cattle, horses and sheep to graze unattended with no shelter and only occasional visits from their herdsmen. In 1997 the remaining sheep were removed from the island and the result has been the regeneration of its vegetation.

Staffa is also a haven for seabirds, with puffin, kittiwake, shag and gulls all nesting on the island, while grey seals, dolphins, basking sharks and even small whales can be found in its surrounding waters.

By contrast, the island of Iona, only 6 miles to the south of Staffa, is composed of entirely different rocks. Its base rock of Laurentian gneiss has been burst through in many places with granite and is also overlaid with quartz, slate and dolomite marble; its soil is fertile. The island is thought to have been already inhabited by the time Saint Columba landed there with twelve followers in AD 563. Already a respected holy man in Ireland and

For most people the voyage to Staffa and Iona began at Oban's North Pier, where they boarded a steamer which sailed to the islands and returned to Oban in the evening. In this Edwardian picture passengers are boarding SS *Grenadier* (on the left with steam up) for what was known as the Sacred Isles tour. The paddle steamer on the right is the SS *Chevalier*, which is working the Oban to Crinan mail service. The small white gabled building above her bows is the Oban Inn, established in 1790 and still there today; next to it on the left is the sandstone end of the Columba Hotel, and the long buildings behind her after-funnel are on the North Pier itself. The Alexandra Hotel can be seen on the left behind the SS *Grenadier*. The SS *Chevalier* was built in 1866 by J. & G. Thomson for the Staffa and Iona service, which she maintained until she was replaced by the SS *Grenadier* in 1885. She then transferred to the Oban–Crinan run which she performed, with an interval during the First World War, until 25 March 1927, when she suffered a catastrophic breakdown. She fractured her starboard paddle wheel during a gale and was blown onto rocks near Barmore Island. Her passengers and mails were landed safely by lifeboat and she was towed to Troon for examination. Unfortunately, repair was considered to be uneconomic in view of her age and she was scrapped there and then.

A panoramic view of Staffa from the south-east as SS *Grenadier* pauses off Fingal's Cave. This paddle steamer was built on Clydebank in 1885 by J. & G. Thomson for David MacBrayne and apart from a spell as a minesweeper during the First World War, she served MacBrayne's for 42 years. On 6 September 1927 a serious fire broke out aboard while she was moored at Oban's North Pier, in which her master, Captain McArthur, and two other seamen lost their lives. Her hulk was towed to Greenock and subsequently to Ardrossan, where she was broken up.

Fingal's Cave is the largest cave on Staffa, being approximately 230 feet long, 60 feet high and 50 feet wide at its entrance. The cave is named after Finn MacCumhaill or McColl, who some say was a legendary giant reputed to have lived in the area in mythological times, while others claim that he was the Celtic equivalent of England's King Arthur. Whatever the truth of the legend, the cave is the most famous feature on Staffa.

This pyramid-shaped little island lies off the east coast of Staffa just to the north-east of Fingal's Cave and is composed entirely of basaltic columns. Its name in Gaelic is Am Buachaille, which means 'The Herdsman'. When the molten lava flows came into contact with the cold bedrock they cooled and contracted into the hexagonal pillars we see today in this picture. The island needs to be seen at low tide to fully appreciate its geological splendour.

In this 1906 photograph a party of tourists on RMS *Iona* have transferred to a rowing boat and are disembarking at the old landing place at the mouth of Fingal's Cave. Luckily for them, the weather is very calm; landing at this spot could not be attempted in any other conditions. In the background, behind the steamer, is the isle of Iona.

On a southerly course down the east side of Staffa, SS *Grenadier* anchors off the Herdsman while her passengers visit Fingal's Cave. Notice the ship's 'clipper'-style bows; although she was built as a modern steamship in 1885, her design was similar to the fast sailing ships known as 'clippers', of which the *Cutty Sark* is the supreme example.

STAFFA, FROM THE SUMMIT. 1134. J.V.

This dramatic picture shows part of the west coast of Staffa at Port an Fhasgaidh. The Gaelic name means 'Shelter Haven' and this area was, in fact, the only part of the island where boats could be pulled up on the beach clear of the surf. It was known locally as 'The Old Harbour'. The top of the island is quite flat and suggestions have been put forward in the past for building a modern tourist hotel or even an aircraft landing strip but, thankfully (in the author's opinion), these proposals have so far come to nothing.

The isle of Iona lies only 6 miles south of Staffa and is our next calling place on the Sacred Isles cruise. It was originally simply called 'I' (pronounced 'ee'), which means island, and it has also been called Icolmkill. Unlike Staffa, it had a proper landing place, constructed in 1850 at Port Ronain, to which passengers could be ferried from the steamer in all but the worst weather. There were no frills about it: passengers disembarked from small open boats onto a stone jetty that was completely exposed to the elements with no shelter of any kind. Even that was a great improvement on the previous arrangement, in which boats landed at Carraig Fhada ('the long rock') on the other side of the small bay and visitors had to make their precarious way ashore. In this photograph two Victorian ladies and a boy, almost camouflaged against the rocks, are enjoying the peaceful atmosphere. The modern landing place is situated just to the left of the old one and the ladies are sitting where the modern vehicle ramp was constructed in 1979. Of the houses in the background, the darker building on the left is no longer there but the row of thatched cottages has survived, although they have been slated and greatly enlarged. The smaller dark building to their right was the old fire station, which still stands today although serving a different purpose.

In 1925 Turbine Steamers Ltd ordered a revolutionary new cruise ship from William Denny & Brothers of Dumbarton. She was powered by six steam turbines and was licensed to carry 814 passengers. Brought into service in 1926, she was named *King George V* and initially her regular run was from Glasgow's Prince's Pier to Inveraray and back via Dunoon, Rothesay and Tighnabruaich. The following year the company was taken over by MacBrayne's and to many thousands of people she, more than any other ship, became synonymous with the Sacred Isles tour. She was withdrawn from this service in 1974 and, ever since, the tourist from Oban has had to take the ferry to Craignure and journey across Mull by coach to reach the Iona ferry from Fionnphort. The ship was sold to Nationwide Transport; they left her in a dry dock in Cardiff for six years before selling her to Bass Charrington Ltd, who intended to convert her into a floating restaurant. Unfortunately she suffered a serious fire on 26 August 1981 while being refurbished and after a further three years her remains were beached opposite Penarth and abandoned to the waves, a sad end for a lovely old ship. In this picture she is landing passengers at Iona in the 1930s.

In the nineteenth century there were no luxuries about the housing on the island. Croft houses would typically be single-storey and constructed in local stone with a thatched roof which was held down with a form of netting. Heavy stones were often suspended from the netting to help to keep it in place in stormy weather. This old photograph of a croft house and outbuildings was taken at Sligineach, a little distance to the south of the landing area, in the mid-1870s. Note the single chimney in the middle of the roof: this suggests that the house may still have been heated by a fire set in the middle of the room.

Seafood Bar Menu

Seafood *(served hot)*

Two Mull Scallops £6.00
With Stornoway Black Pudding served on a bed of mixed Salad.

Three Mull Scallops £6.00
Cooked in Butter and Garlic, served with Salad and Crusty Bread.

Locally Grown Island Mussels *from* £5.00
Cooked in White Wine, Garlic, Onions and Cream.

Locally Caught Langoustines £7.00
Cooked in Garlic and Butter, served whole in the shell on a bed of Salad with Crusty Bread.

Loch Fyne Kippers £3.50
Served warm with Crusty Bread.

Seafood *(served cold)*

Locally Caught Dressed Crab £5.50

Locally Caught Lobster £12.50
Halved and dressed with Prawns, Lobster and White Crab Meat.

Local Langoustines in the Shell £6.00
With Marie Rose Sauce on the side.

Tobermory Hot Smoked Salmon £5.50
With a Chilli Jam Glaze served with Salad and mini Oatcakes.

Tobermory Pâté £3.50
Smoked Mackerel, Salmon or Trout Pâté served with Oatcakes.

Tub of Icelandic Prawns £4.00

Local Whole Cooked Lobster *from* £15.00

Cooked Crab Claws *each* £1.50

Tub of Crab Meat *from* £2.50
White or brown meat.

Oysters *each* £1.00
Served with a slice of Lemon.

The Creel

Speciality Seafood Platter *(ideal for two)* £12.50
Lobster, Crab, Prawns, Salmon, Smoked Salmon, Langoustines and Mussels on a bed of Salad.

Sandwiches

Icelandic Prawns in Marie Rose Sauce £3.50

Locally Caught Crab £3.80
(white or mixed meat)

Lobster in Marie Rose Sauce £5.00

Mull Grown Salmon £3.20

Smoked Salmon and Cream Cheese £3.50

Tuna Mayonnaise £2.50

Salads

Icelandic Prawn Cocktail £5.00

Lobster Cocktail £6.00

White Crab Meat £5.00

Lobster & Langoustine £6.00

Beverages

Tea £1.00

Coffee (filter) £1.50

Hot Chocolate £1.50

Juice (can) £1.00

Juice (bottle) £1.50

Water £1.00

These cottages show a later development from those opposite, now having a fireplace and chimney at each end of the building. Their roofs are still thatched but this is no longer held down with netting. The nearest cottage is inhabited but looks desperately in need of some attention.

IONA HOMESTEADS - JUDGES' LTD.

MV *Lochfyne*, pictured here, was a newer vessel than *King George V*, having been built in 1931 by Denny Brothers of Dumbarton to MacBrayne's order. She was slightly the smaller vessel and not as fast, registering a trial speed of 16.5 knots compared with *King George*'s trial speed of 20.8 knots, but she did have the distinction of being the first British diesel-electric passenger ship. She was not altogether successful, her machinery setting up a vibration that was very noticeable on the passenger decks, and her early career was plagued by a succession of breakdowns, the most spectacular one being on 25 July 1939 when her starboard engine exploded at Oban. During the Second World War she operated the Ardrishaig mail service, sailing from Wemyss Bay because of the anti-submarine boom which stretched across the Clyde estuary throughout the war. She suffered a sad fate in her old age, being disposed of in January 1970 to Northern Slipway Ltd, who used her as a floating generator and accommodation ship at Faslane, before selling her on to Scottish & Newcastle Breweries in 1972. The latter had hoped to convert her into a floating restaurant but soon gave up the attempt and on 25 March 1974 they sent to her to Arnott Young Shipbreakers at Dalmuir on the Clyde to be scrapped.

LANDING AT IONA
PHOTO BY D. B. MAC CULLOCH

MV *Lochfyne* in happier days, landing several boatloads of passengers at Iona. She intermittently shared the summertime Sacred Isles cruise with *King George V* and for the rest of the time she mainly worked the Gourock–Ardrishaig mail service, which had been known as the Royal Route to the Highlands ever since Queen Victoria had used it in 1847. The ship had originally been certificated for nearly 1,200 passengers but this was later reduced to 906. Her two funnels were there to give her an impressive appearance but the forward funnel was, in fact, a dummy!

In 1843 the internal dissensions within the Established (Presbyterian) Church in Scotland led to a massive breakaway of clergy and congregations, who set up the Free Church of Scotland. The minister of Iona, Donald McVean, was one of those who joined the Free Church and consequently was forced to leave his comfortable manse and church and had to rely on the generosity of his congregation to house himself and his family. Initially the island's owner, the Duke of Argyll, was hostile to the Free Church but in 1845 he relented and gave a plot of ground at Martyrs' Bay for a Free Church to be built and gave another plot in the village for a manse. The building in this picture is the 1845 Free Church. When the Free Churches reunited with the Established Church in 1929 to become the Church of Scotland, the island's services were initially held here but after the Established Church's building was extensively refurbished it was decided to make that the parish church. The Free Church building was sold off and was purchased by Dr Isobel Grant in 1935 to house her Highland Folk Museum but this later outgrew the building and in 1939 she relocated it to Kingussie. The church is now a private house named Carraig Beag.

Compared with the view of the same row of cottages on the front cover, this later photograph shows that some of the houses at Baile Mor on Iona were converted into two-storeyed dwellings with dormer windows, and all with slated roofs. The thatched-roofed cottages to the left of the Argyll Hotel have been demolished, and were subsequently replaced by the present-day house named Tigh na Traight. Still moving leftwards, next comes Lovedale Cottage (enlarged with a second storey and dormer windows), followed by Primrose Cottage. The small white cottage, still single-storeyed in 2007, is known as the White House and was the village post office until 1897. The semi-detached house at the far left is Roseneath (right) and Block House (left).

Passing from the village street onto the road that leads towards the abbey, you come first of all to the ruins of the Augustinian nunnery. This view was taken from Cnoc Mor above the nunnery around 1930. RMS *King George V* is lying at anchor in the Sound of Iona, and the Isle of Mull can be seen in the distance with its little village of Fionnphort sheltered in the bay. The Augustinian nunnery was founded in 1203 by Reginald, Lord of the Isles. To its left are the roofless remains of Teampull Ronain (St Ronan's Chapel), which was once the island's parish church. It has since been restored and now houses the nunnery's museum.

When Reginald, Lord of the Isles built the nunnery in 1203, he installed his sister Beatrice as its first prioress. The building was constructed mainly of pink granite which was quarried on Mull and shipped across the water. The arches led from the nave into a side aisle. It was one of only two Augustinian foundations in Scotland and the nuns wore black robes, leading to the church being dubbed 'An Eaglais Dhubh' – the black church. The nunnery was destroyed in 1561 during the Scottish Reformation at the same time as the abbey. No attempt has ever been made to restore it and the pink granite walls of its ruins are an eloquent reminder of the violence of those times. The whole site is now a memorial garden.

This appears to be a guided tour of the nunnery for a party of well-dressed Edwardians. They are probably admiring the tomb of Anna MacLean, the last prioress, who died in the sixteenth century and whose likeness was carved on her tombstone. The carving has survived the centuries so well that even details of her dress can be clearly made out. On her tombstone her head is supported by an angel on each side and above it are a mirror and comb. Clearly prioresses were expected to keep up appearances, even after death! The carving has now been moved indoors to ensure its preservation.

Carved Stones in Nunnery, Iona.

This picture shows four beautifully carved Celtic tombstones which used to be displayed at the side of the doorway between the church and the sacristy at the nunnery. In recent years they have been moved under cover for preservation into the former infirmary and into the cloisters. The nunnery was built as a quadrangle with the church on its north side, the cloister in the centre and the chapter house on the east side. Next to it, St Ronan's Chapel, dating from the same time as the nunnery and now housing the nunnery's museum, contains many of the carved stones that used to be scattered around the precincts.

Maclean's Cross stands at a bend in the road leading up to the abbey. Hewn from mica schist and standing about 11 feet high, the cross is believed to have been commissioned by a member of the Clan Maclean in the latter part of the fifteenth century. The view on the left shows its eastern face, covered with carvings of an intricate Celtic design.

Macleans Cross, Iona

On the western face of Maclean's Cross (shown here and on the right, opposite) is a carving of Christ crucified. Nearby are the church and manse, which were built in 1828 to one of Thomas Telford's 'Parliamentary' designs. This is one of the famous engineer's less well-known activities; at the same time as he was building roads and designing great bridges throughout the kingdom he was also commissioned by the government to design several 'standard' church buildings for the Established (i.e. Presbyterian) Church that could be built throughout the Highlands and Islands. In all, 42 of these were built in the Highlands and Islands, including the one on Iona which, although subsequently modified internally, is externally a typical example of his design.

Two years after the Disruption of 1843, which led to the formation of the Free Church of Scotland, the Duke of Argyll granted land for the Free Church to build a manse in the village for its minister. The manse was completed in 1846 but the Duke did not renew the lease when it expired in 1865 and the minister moved to a newly built house at Achaban, just outside Fionnphort. In 1868 the Duke advertised the former manse to let with 'Two public and six bedrooms. Well adapted for the accommodation of travellers. Well worthy of the attention of persons accustomed to the management of inns or lodging houses.' It was purchased by Captain and Mrs George Ritchie, who were the first of many owners of what became the St Columba Hotel. The rear of the former manse can be seen in the middle foreground of the picture; in the background the SS *Grenadier* waits patiently in the Sound of Iona for her passengers to return from their pilgrimage to the abbey.

ST. COLUMBA HOTEL, IONA
The sheer numbers of visitors to Iona ensured that the St Columba Hotel would need to expand beyond the size of the old manse. This view of the front of the hotel shows how new wings have been added on either side and a veranda has been added to the front, but the original manse can still be recognised in the centre. Over the years the number of bedrooms has been increased to 27, giving accommodation for 45 guests. Since 2005 the hotel has been owned by a small consortium of local people who have formed a company known as St Columba Hotel Ltd.

This view of the abbey shows the Reilig Odhrain, the burial place of the chiefs, with the ruins of St Oran's Chapel and the abbey in the background. The enclosure is named after a monk named Oran, who is said to have accompanied Columba to Iona and who, according to legend, volunteered to be buried alive here as a human sacrifice to sanctify the ground and to ensure that the walls of Columba's new church did not collapse.

206195.JV.

Left: By 1549 the burials of 48 Scottish, 8 Norwegian and 4 Irish kings had been recorded in the Reilig Odhrain. The enclosure includes the graves of Duncan and his alleged murderer, Macbeth, immortalised in Shakespeare's 'Scottish' play. However, Macbeth's conqueror, Malcolm Canmore, chose to be buried at Dunfermline Abbey and subsequently only one more Scottish king was buried on Iona.

Right: The tombs of the Macleans were also prominent within the Reilig Odhrain. One of these belonged to Maclaine of Lochbuy, known as Ewen of the Little Head, who is depicted buckling on his sword. His ghost is said still to revisit his family, riding on a black horse. Another is of Maclean of Duart, who is wearing armour with a shield on his left shoulder depicting a dragon and tower. He holds a spear in his left hand and is standing on a greyhound. Like all the other gravestones in the Reilig Odhrain, they have now been moved under cover into the safety of the abbey precincts.

IONA CATHEDRAL, (INTERIOR). 784

This picture shows part of the devastation to the abbey resulting from the Scottish Reformation of 1560 when its roof was stripped of lead and its treasures ransacked. It remained in this state for over 300 years.

St Oran's Chapel, close by the abbey, was probably built by either Reginald himself or his father Somerled, as a family burial chamber in the middle of the twelfth century. It is the oldest intact building on the island and was the burial place of the Lords of the Isles until the sixteenth century. Somerled and his successors ruled over a huge portion of Scotland, and his grandson, Donald, was the founder of the great Clan MacDonald. The chapel was restored in 1957 but these photographs show it in its earlier ruinous state. The photograph on the far right was taken in 1930 after some 'tidying' of the doorway and chapel had taken place. This doorway shows Irish influences in its architecture with its carvings incorporating chevrons and beaked heads, and inside on the right is a tomb recess which is thought to have been built by John, the last Lord of the Isles, who died in 1503. The recess would have been built to house his tomb and effigy. Since restoration the gravestones seen here on the ground have been lifted and are displayed inside the chapel along its left-hand wall.

St Oran's Chapel, Io

DOORWAY ST ORAN'S CHAPEL, IONA CATHEDRAL.

The original St John's Cross, on the right dates, from the tenth century or even earlier. It has a span of more than 7 feet, which proved too ambitious for a carving in stone. It was originally constructed as a plain cross without any support for the arms, but it was soon found necessary to strengthen it with four segments of stone ring, turning it into the usual Celtic style so familiar today. Even so, the cross had an unfortunate history. It apparently collapsed soon after its strengthening; even in modern times and despite being renovated in 1926, it was blown down in fierce gales in both 1951 and 1957. Since then the fragments of the original cross have been taken into the abbey museum, and a concrete replica (shown below) has stood in its place since 1970.

IONA CATHEDRAL AND ST, MARTINS CROSS. 781. J,V.

This closer view of the abbey shows just how little remained of its buildings after the ravages of 1561. One of the few Celtic crosses to survive intact was St Martin's Cross, which stands to this day on the western side of the abbey. It was hewn from a slab of grey epidiorite stone brought from Argyll and is set in a base of red granite. It is believed to have been constructed between AD 759 and AD 800. It has beautiful carvings depicting the Virgin and Child, scenes from the Old Testament and intertwined serpents, and its eastern face (not shown here) displays carvings of bosses and serpents. St Martin, as well as being the fourth-century patron saint of France, was a friend of St Ninian and was venerated in the Scottish and Irish churches. His name was invoked in the prayers of the liturgy used in Iona by St Columba himself. This view contrasts with the picture of the restoration of the abbey, shown on p. 6.

SACRISTY DOOR, IONA CATHEDRAL.
NO. I.

The empty windows behind the site of the high altar tell their own story in the Victorian photograph above. In pre-Reformation days they were filled with stained-glass images of the Catholic saints but these were destroyed by the Presbyterian reformers in 1561. The choir and chancel in this picture date largely from the sixteenth-century rebuilding of the abbey. At the time of this photograph the abbey had no roof and the effects of centuries of Scottish weather can be seen on the walls. Note the sacristy door on the left; before 1500 this area was a crypt and the floor of the church was level with the top of the door. Around 1500 the ceiling of the crypt was removed and the area was opened out. A portion of the north aisle was converted into a sacristy, where the abbey's vestments and sacramental vessels used during services were kept and this elaborate doorway was constructed to give access to it. Its weathered appearance shows the effects of five centuries of exposure to the elements between the time the abbey was plundered in 1561 and its restoration in the twentieth century, as shown in the post-restoration view on the left. The picture above shows that the area above the door used to be walled up but this was opened out during the restoration of the abbey. The space above the door is now crowned by pointed arches.

EAST END OF NAVE IONA CATHEDRAL.
11038.J.V.
In 1899 the 8th Duke of Argyll, the owner of the island, gave the ruins of the abbey to the Iona Cathedral Trust, who immediately set about raising public subscriptions to restore the abbey church. Restoration work on the church began in 1902 and was completed in 1910. One of the first areas to be restored was the east end by the site of the high altar. This photograph, showing the window restored, albeit with plain glass, contrasts markedly with the picture opposite. The new altar was constructed out of marble quarried from the south-east corner of the island. The gravestones leaning against the wall below the window are now displayed in the adjacent cloisters.

IONA CATHEDRAL, S. AISLE. 1897 J.V.

This view of the abbey's south aisle shows its unusual construction, owing to the original thirteenth-century structure being rebuilt and enlarged in the fifteenth century and again in the seventeenth century.

Two Edwardian tourists rest in the shade of St Martin's Cross, here showing the intricate carvings on the east side. The photograph on the right was taken in the 1960s.

In 1938 the Iona Community was founded by the Rev. George Macleod, a parish priest in Glasgow. His aim was to set up an ecumenical Christian community committed to seeking new ways of living the gospel in the modern world through ministry and mission work throughout Scotland and beyond. Their work began with the restoration of the remaining ruined monastic buildings of the abbey. This took until the mid-1960s to complete, and this photograph, taken when the project was nearing completion, shows the magnificent result. The island of Mull, seen across the Sound of Iona, provides an inspiring backdrop.

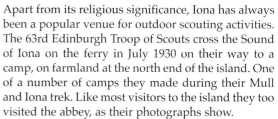

Apart from its religious significance, Iona has always been a popular venue for outdoor scouting activities. The 63rd Edinburgh Troop of Scouts cross the Sound of Iona on the ferry in July 1930 on their way to a camp, on farmland at the north end of the island. One of a number of camps they made during their Mull and Iona trek. Like most visitors to the island they too visited the abbey, as their photographs show.

Above: The scouts didn't have the farmland all to themselves; they had to share their field with their hosts' Highland cattle. The cattle look happy and docile enough in this photograph but I wonder if they ever tried eating raw Boy Scouts as a change from grass? The campsite appears to have been situated on the north-west corner of the island near Calva, looking out towards Eilean Chalbha.

Right: The Macdonald family, photographed by the Scouts in 1930. Perhaps the Scouts were camping on their land.

Left: Rock climbing can be hazardous at any time but the added risk of climbing on a windy day while wearing a kilt adds another dimension to the adventure. Let us hope that the climber reached the top of Dun-I, the principal hill on the island, without suffering any permanent damage to his faculties.

Below: Even on a sunny July day the waters around Mull and Iona can be very chilly but these Edinburgh scouts must have been a hardy lot. One of their maxims was 'Cleanliness is next to Godliness', and a daily bathe was compulsory. Judging from their happy faces they seem to have enjoyed their dip in the sea.

All good things must come to an end sometime. Here the Edinburgh scouts are striking camp at the end of their summer holiday on Iona. One of the tents is already down but there still appear to be a lot of heavy cooking utensils to be stowed away somewhere.

The lads look in fine form on their return journey to Mull and onward to the mainland. Being an inland troop located in Edinburgh, a week's camping in the fresh air on Iona would have done them the world of good.

Calva is an agricultural area in the north-west of Iona. Although it is now uninhabited, the remains of earlier cultivation can be seen, along with the foundations of croft houses. The beauty of sunsets over the Western Isles of Scotland is legendary. This tranquil picture of the area at sunset is looking out to the small islands of Eeilran Chalba.

MULL, FROM DUN I IONA.

Dun-I is the only real hill on Iona. It is only 332 feet high and can be easily climbed from the road just beyond the abbey (provided you are wearing suitable footwear) and the views from its summit can be magnificent. This view is looking north-east towards Mull with the small island of Eilean Annraidh lying just beyond the headland, and the white sands of Caolas Annraidh shining between them. On a clear day you can see northwards to Staffa and beyond it to the islands of Coll, Tiree, Barra, Rhum, Eigg and the Treshnish Islands, while to the south you can see Colonsay, Islay and the Paps of Jura.

On the summit of Dun-I is a cairn which was built in 1897 to commemorate Queen Victoria's Diamond Jubilee. Nearby there is a pool named Tobar na h-Aois (the Well of Age), in which youthfulness is said to be magically restored if you bathe in it three times as the sun rises. More practically, lower down the hill is a boggy area known as Lon a' Phoit Dhubh (Meadow of the Black Pot) where illicit whisky stills used to be hidden when Excise men were on the prowl.

Continuing down the west coast of Iona and heading southwards, we come to a unique inlet where the rocks are shaped in such a way that the incoming tide dashing into them can throw a vertical plume of water a hundred feet into the air. This is known locally as Uamh an t-Seididh – the Spouting Cave.

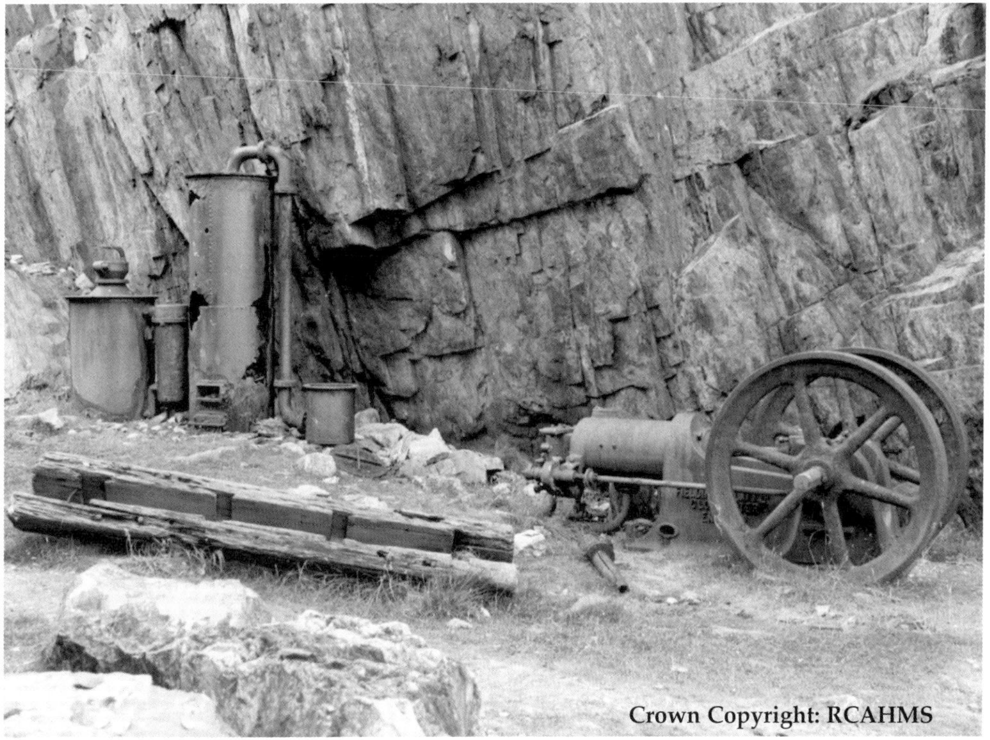

Continuing round to the south-east coast of the island, there is an outcrop of forsterite tremolite marble which is mainly white in colour but streaked with light green serpentine. The marble was first quarried here in medieval times and the abbey's first altar was carved from it. The quarry extends about 100 yards inland but the marble has always been expensive to extract and transport. In the 1700s the Duke of Argyll attempted to market Iona marble in a number of affluent European cities but had to give up because of the cost. The picture on the left shows blocks of marble that have been hewn from the quarry and abandoned. The local belief was that the marble not only possessed healing powers but that its possession also gave protection against shipwreck, fire and miscarriage. When the abbey was wrecked by the Reformers in 1561, the local people began chipping away small pieces of the altar to carry around as protection, and visitors did the same for souvenirs. When Johnson and Boswell visited the ruins in 1773 they noted that the altar had completely disappeared in this way!

After it had been left abandoned for many years, another attempt was made in 1907 to operate the quarry. Once again the project was found to be unviable and operations ceased at the time of the First World War. The floor of St Andrew's Chapel in London's Westminster Cathedral contains marble quarried from Iona during this period. The quarry itself, together with its machinery, was abandoned and the whole ghostly site is now scheduled as an Ancient Monument. The picture on the right shows a horizontal gas engine manufactured by Messrs Fielding & Platt of Gloucester, which has lain rusting in the quarry for nearly a century.

The farm of Traighmor lies at the southern tip of the belt of farmland that runs from the northern end of the island down its east coast and it is enclosed by rocky ground on three sides. A gaggle of geese from the farm is exploring the meadow in front of a row of beehive-shaped hayricks at the foot of the rocks.

Victorian tourists return to SS *Grenadier* after visiting the island sometime around 1890; a second boatload of passengers can be seen in the distance already disembarking onto the cruise ship.

The departing visitors' last view of Iona. The large building on the right is the Bishop's House, which was built as a guest house by the Episcopal Church in 1894, where visitors can spend a retreat in a Christian environment. It caused a great deal of controversy at the time among the mainly Presbyterian inhabitants of the island, but this was overcome. In 1897 over 600 Roman Catholic pilgrims came by a special steamer to say mass on the 1300th anniversary of St Columba's death. On this occasion three separate denominational services were held but subsequently the island became more ecumenical in its religious worship. The white house to the left of the Bishop's House is Lorne Cottage and next to it is the house called Erraid. The building on the extreme left of the picture is the Highland Cottage.